PANORAMA
of
CREATION

All scripture references are from the King James Version unless otherwise stated.

PANORAMA OF CREATION
© 1989, 1992 by Creation Evidences Museum

Printed in the United States of America

Published by
Bible Belt Publishing
P.O. Box 100 • Bethany, OK 73008 • 1-800-652-1144

ISBN 1-879366-01-0

PANORAMA
of
CREATION

Carl E. Baugh, Ph.D.

To the Creator whose work we enjoy

Dr. Baugh is completing a new book for 1997, *Creation in Symphony.* This work enlarges on the concepts of this book and gives full technical support.

Dr. Baugh's accredited degrees (plus his doctoral dissertation) are available on our internet home page:

http://www.texoma.com/~linesden/cem/

Table of Contents

Chapter One

Orchestration Involves a Young Earth

In this book we will be reporting on research that we have been doing at the Creation Evidences Museum in Glen Rose, Texas. More than forty scientists have participated during the last seven years in a research project at Glen Rose. We have uncovered a major Acrocanthosaurus dinosaur. We are in the process of building an enormous hyperbaric biosphere. We are also building a $1/_{20}$th scale model of Noah's Ark.

During our research for these projects, we have been doing extensive studies on the creation model. In this book I shall attempt to give you an overview of the first composite creation model that, to our knowledge, has ever been presented. We call it, "Creation in Symphony."

There is a very special reason for the term "Creation in Symphony." From the Word of God we find a definite indication that all of the physical creation was designed, or "orchestrated," for man, who was made in the image of God. All of the days of creation were a buildup to the finale, which was the creation of the creature made in the image of God, and his companion, woman, who was made to walk by his side and meet his needs. The biblical record is clear, for Jesus said, "But from the beginning of the creation God made them male and female" (Mark 10:6). This verse says a number of things to us.

First of all, it says that the universe is not sixteen and a half billion years old. It says that the Earth is not four and a half billion years old. God specified that in ". . . the beginning of the creation God made them male and female." God has existed eternally. In His record He gave us a very clear exposure of factors in this creation.

From the beginning of the creation, we can then point back to the history of man in majestic life form. Man came on the stage fully operational, with the ability to accomplish all that God designed for him to accomplish. Man was in communication with himself, with his environment, and with his Creator. From the beginning of creation we can trace the history of man.

This infers another concept. Man and woman were made on the sixth day of creation. It was not until after that sixth day that the Bible says, "It is finished." So the entire creation was made in a progressive form in a matter of six days, yet the time scale for that physical six-day creation is "the beginning." We have the phrase used in the Word of God, "Jesus Christ, the beginning, the author and finisher of our faith." Here we have the God-Man as the beginning of this physical creation, meaning that all of the creation is orchestrated for His benefit— and the benefit of those He created.

There is a special word that scientists have conceptualized which speaks of this particular facet. It is the word *anisotrophy*. This means that as you observe the physical creation and the complexity of life from the amoeba through tiny amphibians, reptiles, avian creatures (the birds of the air), and other complicated life forms, you also observe that man is the repertoire of the physical creation. The brain of man is the most sophisticated, complicated device ever observed in the entire physical universe.

Man is the repository of the goodness of God, made in the image of God, reflecting God's goodness and capacity to love, to examine right and wrong, virtue and evil. God designed man as the ultimate form of His physical creation. Then God breathed into his nostrils the breath of life, and man became a living soul. Man is more than simply a biological creature. He is a living soul, a direct descendant of the attributes of Almighty God in immediate form. Man did not evolve; man was given all of these capacities instantly.

All that we observe appears to complement the existence for man: the orchestrated world about us, the ecosphere, and the stellarsphere. That is the concept that we are presenting. This orchestrated creation was made for the benefit of man, and required the hand of Almighty God.

The days of creation were literal. Let's begin in Genesis chapter 1.

> In the beginning God created the heaven and the earth. And the earth was without form, and void; and darkness was upon the face of the deep. And the Spirit of God moved upon the face of the waters. And God said,

> Let there be light: and there was light. And God saw
> the light, that it was good: and God divided the light
> from the darkness. And God called the light Day, and
> the darkness he called Night. And the evening and the
> morning were the first day. And God said, Let there be
> a firmament in the midst of the waters, and let it di-
> vide the waters from the waters. And God made the
> firmament, and divided the waters which were under
> the firmament from the waters which were above the
> firmament: and it was so. And God called the firma-
> ment Heaven. And the evening and the morning were
> the second day. (vss. 1–8)

The description of the days of creation continue. We read
in Genesis 1:14-19.

> And God said, Let there be lights in the firmament of
> the heaven to divide the day from the night; and let
> them be for signs, and for seasons, and for days, and
> years: And let them be for lights in the firmament of
> the heaven to give light upon the earth: and it was so.
> And God made two great lights; the greater light to
> rule the day, and the lesser light to rule the night: he
> made the stars also. And God set them in the firma-
> ment of the heaven to give light upon the earth, And
> to rule over the day and over the night, and to divide
> the light from the darkness: and God saw that it was
> good. And the evening and the morning were the
> fourth day.

A repetitive phrase given again and again is, "the evening
and the morning." I've been asked repeatedly why, if God

created man and the entire universe in literal days, did He begin with night instead of day? There is a profound reason for this that we have anticipated in our research.

First of all, God used the Hebrew mind to display the revelation of His Word. The Hebrew language is, essentially, the most perfect language known to man. The Greek language has broader expression, but the Hebrew language is basic and fundamental to the concepts of life. The Hebrew mind begins the day with the night; that is, the succeeding day begins at six o'clock the preceding evening. But, of course, the Hebrews got that idea from God. Why does God begin with night?

We think the answer is simply this: God begins with nothing but night and silence. By His special, immediate, direct creative ability (which is limited only to His own desire), God, out of nothing, creates light, beauty, and life. We in turn take that beauty, life, and light with a bright day and turn it into night. We begin with a day and it closes into night. God begins with night and nothing, and creates that which brings glory unto Himself.

The emphasis in the Hebrew text is that the creation days are literal. The word *Yom* is used in the Hebrew, and unless there is a specific contextual arrangement, it always means a literal day. How is it possible for these six days of creation and the seventh day of rest to be literal days?

Initially, the reason the days of creation had to be literal is because of the interrelationship of life. On day number one, God created light and He created the Earth. In fact, He began by creating the Earth. The Earth was there by His special, direct, creative hand—a display of majesty and power. On day number two, God accomplished a special work and created a firmament. We will give special attention to the creation of the firmament in succeeding chapters. And then, on day number three, God created the rest of the elements, the "terra firma," both within and on the surface of the Earth; He also created the life forms that we call "botanical," the vegetation. On day number four, He created the stellar heavens. On day number five, God created the fish and the fowl. On day number six, we find God created the great dinosaurs; they did exist with man before the flood and for a short time afterward. God created the crickets, the butterflies, the dragonflies, and the fireflies. He created the mammals, and the remaining beasts of the field. Then God culminated His special activity by creating man. He created man with a special relationship to his environment, even using the clay from which to fashion a body for man. Before the day was out, God created woman as well.

Chapter Two

Recent Creation—
A Better Explanation

In the theoretical dogma of the evolutionary concept, the lower life forms developed into higher life forms. This is a total contradistinction to what is found in the Word of God. The scenario is entirely different. God's work is distinctive, but there is another very special interplay.

There are some sincere students of the Bible who believe God used ages for days. Instead of the days of creation being literal, some propose that perhaps the days were actually ages—perhaps thousands of years, perhaps millions of years, and some have envisioned even billions of years. They have attempted to force the text of the Scripture to support this notion. Scripture, however, does not support such a concept.

It was on day number three that God created the botanical life forms. It was not until day number four that God created the stellar heavens—the sun and the moon— to create the ability for photosynthesis. If the Earth were enshrouded in a cloud of darkness, there would not have been the ability for photosynthesis until the sun and more of the stellar heavens were visible and usable as light sources. In a matter of forty-eight hours, most of the botanical life forms would be dead. In a matter of twenty-eight days, all of them would be dead without the ability, designed by the Lord, that the stellar bodies give for photosynthesis upon the Earth.

Even if that were not the case, it was not until day number six that God created the insects that are so very important to the procreation of most of these botanical life forms. There is such an interplay of the life forms that the days of creation have to be literal days. Let us examine this concept even further.

The Earth's electromagnetic field has been found by Dr. Thomas Barnes to be decreasing exponentially, losing one-half of its energy every fourteen hundred years. If we extrapolate, and turn the clock backward (as weak as the field is today, causing such problems as depletion of the ozone layer with increased exposure to ultraviolet radiation) this means that fourteen hundred years ago it was twice as strong as it is today. This also means that twenty-eight hundred years ago, the Earth's electromagnetic field was four times as strong as it is today. When you go back in time beyond eight to ten thousand years, you find the electromagnetic field of the Earth would have been so powerful that the existence of life would have been impossible. Many fine physicists have run calculations to show that if you extend as far back as fifteen thousand years, the energy of the Earth's magnetic field would approximate that of a magnetic star. Under such conditions, it would have been impossible for life as we know it to exist on the Earth. So, when we take the literal facts, we find that we don't have thousands and millions of years to deal with in relation to this intercontext of the days of creation. Now, let us explore another dimension.

The sun is losing energy. It is giving up energy in this orchestrated design for man and for the solar system. It is losing a certain number of feet per hour in surface material. If you extrapolate back several tens of thousands of years, this means that the sun would have been appreciably larger, which means that the Earth would have been scorched. It also means that the gravitational pull of the sun upon the Earth would have caused the Earth to catapult into the sun. This again proves that you really don't have a lot of time to deal with. Let's consider another directive.

The moon is receding from the Earth a few inches each year. It would seem that there is a lot of space to play with, as there are approximately two hundred thirty thousand miles separating the Earth from the moon. But if you extend time back many tens of thousands of years, this means that the moon would have been so close to the Earth that all of Earth's continents would be covered with water twice a day! Again, this shows that everything was meticulously and artistically designed. It was orchestrated at the beginning.

When our space probes were sent to Saturn, the mission discovered a very unique thing in their observations. It was found that the rings of Saturn are actually intertwined. They appear to be braided. All the laws of physics show that after several tens of thousands of years, this intertwining of the rings would have been lost, and the rings would have amalgamized to the point where they were relatively uniform in composition. This means that Someone designed them in their braided form just a few thousand years ago.

Now, let us address a difficult issue. From the pressure of oil wells, it appears that the Earth is just a few thousand years old. From observations of the near heavens, it appears that the Earth is just a few thousand years old. How then is it possible that there are elements in the rock, such as radioisotopes, which indicate an Earth age of millions, and in some instances, billions of years?

Here is a plausible explanation. There is no data scientifically known which can give a rock a uniform age. All of the processes for dating radioisotopic material and alpha particle decay known to science give a variant in age determination when various portions of the same rock are examined. In other words, scientists really don't have the formula worked out yet.

When the alpha particle decay rate is examined, which is the interpretive line of measurement, it is found that it takes uranium-238 over four billion years to lose half its mass. The line of reasoning goes that it had to have been around for at least four and a half billion years to have lost that much mass. This is not necessarily so. It really shows that U-238 was designed to be around for billions of years, and it was designed to be here for a useful purpose, orchestrated for the benefit of man. In the forthcoming chapters, we will address this issue, and show you why we find the current context of these isotopes on the surface of the Earth.

It is obvious from the geophysicists that these isotopes were, at one time, inside the Earth. They were expunged, or thrown out, to the surface of the Earth. What this demonstrates is that the interior of the Earth, at some time in the past, was a perfectly balanced thermonuclear heater. If these isotopic elements are so arranged with moderating elements adjacent to them, the result is simply a controlled nuclear reactor. God designed the interior of the Earth as such for the benefit of man.

Some stars appear to be billions of light years away. Astrophysicists will admit that the formula which indicates long ages for the stars, known as "the red shift" or "the doppler effect," is in error. The problem is that if we take the formula at face value, on Monday, Wednesday, and Friday, the universe is twice as large as it is on Tuesday, Thursday, and Saturday; and on Sunday, it's a toss-up. That has profound implications. Recently a scientist on the East Coast found that the doppler effect can actually be a phenomenon of the tiring light, rather than suggesting an implication of long-age.

All of these things point to the fact that the entire Earth, ecosystem, and universe were orchestrated in design for the benefit of man—orchestrated by a personal, compassionate God.

In chapter one, we presented the concept of how a loving God, who has encompassed all of the universe through eternity, orchestrated the entire physical creation for the benefit of man. If this is true, and the biblical record certainly asserts this to be true from Genesis through Revelation, and if the days of creation are literal and the creation is recent, this concept runs in direct and diametric opposition to the concept of humanistic evolution. We today are encouched with the concept of humanistic evolution.

Evolutionists believe that all things have occurred by

natural processes. The gods of evolution are time, chance, and natural circumstance. However, it is very interesting to note that the evolutionist is plagued by paranoia. Since at one time this author was an evolutionist, I understand fairly well the mind-set of the evolutionist.

The evolutionist is plagued with an immediate observation that the universe is somewhat in chaos. He interprets this as the second law of thermodynamics, which states that everything is increasing in random order, from complex to less complex. Actually, this second law of thermodynamics demands that there had to have been a time in the past when everything was in perfect synchronization; that is, orchestral creation. But an evolutionist who is a philosophical, or thinking, evolutionist responds to the idea of deterioration of the universe, or a universe in disharmony. The evolutionist first finds this disharmony within himself; then he studies the biological world about him; he studies the stellar heavens; he assimilates all of the data; and he discovers that there is a marked discord. Thus, he literally responds and finds himself in harmony with an inharmonious universe. He is in harmony with a life in conflict. If the evolutionist would consider the evidence, this is exactly what the unique biblical record addresses.

Biblical Christianity, and the Judeo-Christian concept of revelation, is unique in all the world. It is unique in the annals of religions; it is unique in philosophic concept; and it is unique in scientific research. All of the great founders of the discipline of science were literal creationists. Later, the humanistic concept took over the universities and replaced the concepts observed originally by the creationists.

We find an immediate conflict between the concepts of creation and evolution. Many have considered that evolution is a proven fact. Particularly, press releases emphasize this concept. But for those involved in the cutting edge of scientific research, in their admissions privately and sometimes publicly, evolution is far from being a proven fact. What we find is really just the opposite. We find information that shows all of life to be extremely complicated. Let's consider a scientific analysis.

It has been postulated that the universe is about thirty billion light years across. It appears that the Earth is the relative center of the universe. If for sixteen and a half billion years light has been receding from this central point, we can assume the universe would be about thirty-one or thirty-two billion lights years across.

Certainly, the universe's size is dictated by God's perfect plan. We do not believe that the universe is really that large; but for the sake of discussion, let's agree that it is. Scientists have been able to give an assimilative number to the amount of exponential bits of information contained in that total inorganic, nonliving universe. It comes to two hundred thirty-five exponential bits of information. These bits are not to be confused with computer bits, but are a compound bit assimilation. Yet, the human cell has over twenty billion exponential bits of information in its three-dimensional composite. In other words, it is absolutely impossible for the inorganic universe to have produced the human cell. The least complex cell, a simple bacterium, has about seven million exponential bits of information. It is absolutely impossible for this inorganic universe to have produced one living cell of any structure in any biological observation.

What this really means is that life had to be designed, and it appeared fully functional and fully operational.

Even the stars appeared fully operational at the beginning of the creation. One of the concepts of evolutionary consideration is that some of the stars appear to be at times about sixteen billion light years away. At other times, these stars appear to be much closer. The formula which calculates these distances is by no means proven. But even if God wanted them to be sixteen billion light years away, that's no problem for an omnipotent, personal God.

In our computer generation, we find that once the data is entered into a computer, that computer can actually begin at the end or middle of a printout. The computer can work in either or both directions, as long as there is the total knowledge of where all the digits and characters will be placed ultimately. We humans, in our finite consideration and conceptualization, can design and build computers and printing stations capable of printing texts in any direction necessary. Certainly it stands to reason then, that an all-wise God who designed and is in total control of the universe, can know where every particle of matter and energy is to be at any given time. He created a mature universe.

Many evolutionists have opposed the creation concept by saying, "God, in your concept, made the Earth and the universe with age." This is not true. Let's examine the statement using particular schematics. God did not create the universe with age. Adam was fully mature and fully operational when he was created, probably with an appearance of a man approximating the age of twenty-six to thirty years. Yet, while he was fully mature, he was only two minutes old. Time for man began the moment God breathed into his nostrils the breath of life and he became a living soul. He had no age until that moment, yet he was fully mature.

The universe reflects this same experience. There is no age in the universe until the moment of creation, but there is a mature, full-blown operation. It is a "mature" universe, not an "old" universe. It is not the appearance of age, but the immediate observation of maturity. Hopefully, this will settle a problem in the minds of many of the readers.

Let's now address the conflict between the concepts of creation and evolution. When we examine the data available, and take the verified facts into consideration, there is no way the evolutionary paradigm could have occurred. The evolutionary paradigm is the geologic column which supposes that life began to evolve approximately six hundred million years ago in the Cambrian period of the Mesozoic era, and then continued in its complex climb in the Mesozoic era of the great reptiles, or dinosaurs. Supposedly, life continued in ever-increasing complexity with some mysterious force driving it, or through some intellectual capacity written into a universe, such as pantheism envisions. The two concepts of evolution and pantheism are interchangeable in many respects. The supposition continues that life became even more complex in the Cenozoic era. Finally, at the top of the geologic column, man arrived on the scene about two and one-half million years ago. *Homo sapiens* arrived on the scene a few tens of thousands of years ago. *Homo sapiens,* or modern intelligent man, was seen to have evolved according to the concept of evolution. When we examine the actual facts, however, this concept is absolutely impossible.

First of all, the trilobites of this early Cambrian period of the Mesozoic era appear immediately. One outstanding geologist, who headed a department of a major university, admitted some years ago that since the trilobites are found in complex form, the evolutional processes designed them. If they arrived here by time, chance, and natural circumstances, nine-tenths of the geologic column is missing. He observed that there has really been little change within life forms since then. The trilobites appear with complicated eyes. Paleontologists have admitted trilobites have eyes that are so sophisticated that modern cameras are designed paralleling the trilobite. However, trilobites appear immediately in the geologic column. It is absolutely impossible for this to have occurred if evolutionary processes had designed such complicated individual life forms. Now, let's examine some other records.

In a 1982 *Reader's Digest* publication, "The Mysteries of the Unexplained," it was related that a century ago, a very phenomenal thing occurred. If this record is correct, and having so many other anomalies, we certainly do not doubt this account (also, it was related in a verifiable publication), this means it is absolutely impossible for evolution to be the explanation of how life forms got here.

The article refers to the last of the great pterodactyls, the flying dinosaurs of the Mesozoic era. They existed supposedly around one hundred million years ago in the Cretaceous period of the Mesozoic era. The record states that in France, some workmen in the winter of 1856, while working on a partially completed railway tunnel between St. Dizey and the Nancy lines, came across something unusual. In the tunnel they had broken and removed a huge boulder of Jurassic limestone, which precedes the Cretaceous by several million years. After they had broken the limestone, stumbling out of the tunnel toward them was a creature which fluttered its wings, croaked, and collapsed dead at their feet. This creature had a wingspan of ten feet, seven inches, with four legs joined by a membrane like a bat. What should have been feet were long talons. The mouth was arrayed with sharp teeth. The skin was black, leathery, oily, and thick. Local students of paleontology immediately identified this creature as being a pterodactyl. This was all reported in the *Illustrated London News*, February 9, 1856, page 156. They examined the limestone from which the creature had been released and found there a cavity in the exact mold of the creature's body. If this is true, it is absolutely impossible for that creature to have lived more than a few thousand years in any form in hibernation. It would have been impossible for it to have lived more than a few thousand years under those circumstances. The worldwide, biblical Noahic flood explains this phenomenon far better than the evolutionary process.

Let's examine some new data resulting from exhaustive research that the author has been compiling for many years. The biblical record shows before the flood there was a need for great flying reptiles and the great master dinosaurs to keep the vegetation in check in the lush environment. Man was already complete in a sophisticated form. Man began at the top of the column. Man began genetically engineered, totally viable, and totally in harmony with his ecosystem. All of his characteristics were superior.

Chapter Three

Superior Man
from the Beginning

Anthropologists and sociologists admit that if man has certain characteristics, he has to be sophisticated. It is an amazing fact that man from Adam to Noah possessed a composite of approximately fifty-six characteristics that have never, from Noah's time until the present, been possessed by a single culture of man. What this means is that original man was a superior man. Let's examine a list of the superior characteristics that mankind possessed.

1. **Conceptual Analysis:** "And Adam gave names to all cattle, and to the fowl of the air, and to every beast of the field; but for Adam there was not found an help meet for him." That specific names were given to all varieties of separate groups with emphasis on distinctions among them, requires the ability to conceptualize objectively. In order to determine that none of the individuals under consideration would be inti-

mately compatible with the observer further enhances the evidence that the observer had mature self-awareness and mental powers.

2. **Comparative Observation:** ". . . gave names to all cattle . . . and to every beast of the field. . . ." Not only is there distinction made between groups, but comparison and nomenclature is assigned accordingly.

3. **Observational Articulation:** ". . . gave names to all cattle. . . ." Cattle are observed, named, and seen as being categorically separate from undomesticable beasts of the field. Those assigned names were articulated and memorialized for ongoing generations. "Whatsoever Adam called every living creature, that was the name thereof." Such deliberate memorializing for future generations requires sequential listing, even if only by memory.

4. **Synergistic Language:** "And Adam said, this is now bone of my bones, and flesh of my flesh. . . ." Languages which use enlarged expression, enhanced by immediate preceding statements, require complicated emotional and mental functions. The nature of the recorded expression entails a common genetic makeup in contradistinction to the other life forms mentioned, known at least by the writer of the manuscript and known by surface value of the text to Adam, the person making the statement. Common contradistinctive genetic makeup has only been known within recent years by our generation. Functional knowledge among the ancients surpassed the commonly held view among anthropologists.

5. **Speech Anatomy:** ". . . leave his father and mother, and shall cleave. . . ." The complicated structure of

the larynx system and the ability of the oral muscles to frame these words far surpasses commonly held views regarding developing man, such as Neanderthal or Cro-Magnon.

6. **Parallel Expression:** ". . . bone of my bones . . ." ". . . flesh of my flesh . . ." ". . . called Woman [from man] . . ." ". . . taken out of man . . ." ". . . leave his father and mother . . ." ". . . cleave unto his wife . . ." ". . . they shall be one flesh" [repeats concept of common flesh as first mentioned in parallelism]. This form of poetry and complicated expression reveals a highly developed ability in expression.

7. **Poetic Declamation:** Not only is this a form of complicated poetic expression, but it is a progressive statement encompassing origin, state, and destiny of the speaking person (Adam) and the audience (Woman) to be heard and observed by future generations (Father and Mother). Developing man is totally incapable of this speech form.

8. **Domestic Attachment:** "They shall be one flesh." Monogamy and union are expressed and pronounced in the declamation. Filial and romantic ties are strongly suggested.

9. **Domestic Orientation:** ". . . knew Eve his wife." Position and physical union are both expressed in an oriented sense. Father, mother, and child are listed by name.

10. **Incident Reference:** ". . . knew . . . conceived . . . have gotten a man. . . ." A conscious reference is made to physical relations, conception, and birth. Detailed sensitivities are honorably expressed with a deliberate emphasis on time and events.

11. **Occupational Distinction:** "Abel was a keeper of

sheep, but Cain was a tiller of the ground." This concept exposes more than a casual reference to occupation. In short expression we are given names, occupations, and job descriptions. "Keeper" and "tiller" are in correct reference to their appropriate occupations.

12. **Time Perspective:** ". . . tiller of the ground . . . in process of time . . . brought of the fruit of the ground. . . ." Recognition of time, cultivation, and harvest requires sophistication and concept. Man is again seen as being mature, sensitive, and competent.

13. **Environmental Cultivation:** ". . . tiller of the ground. . . ." Anthropologists agree that mature man is the only creature which can deliberately alter his environment. Deliberate cultivation for harvesting purposes is clearly described, requiring concept and intent.

14. **Religious Preoccupation:** ". . . brought an offering unto the Lord." Religious exercise is ascribed to man alone. Conscious religious activity with a specific offering to a specific God is described.

15. **Conceptual Anarchy:** "Cain was very wroth . . . and the Lord said. . . ." The related expression is that of anger to the point of vindictive action against the established authority.

16. **Emotional Response (Negative):** ". . . and his countenance fell." Displayed emotional response to a person relating to an event in time followed by consequences of that response can only be interpreted in the light of cultured man.

17. **Criminal Propensity (Individual):** "Cain rose up against Abel his brother, and slew him." Meaningful commentary is given with insight into individual moral shortfall. Anthropologists view morality and

accountability to have developed very late in man's descent. Social anthropologists recognize criminal propensity as being the experience of truly modern man.

18. **Guilt Consciousness:** "My punishment is greater than I can bear." Modern sophistication and sensitivities are in view in a very ancient context. Knowledge that this guilt complex would follow in his experience for years authenticates the text as being more than embellished writing.

19. **Moral Designation:** ". . . whosoever slayeth Cain, vengeance shall be taken on him sevenfold." Moral responsibility to a person and consequences in the event of failure are clearly defined. Protection and restriction relating the guilty person are also enforced. This describes sophisticated structure.

20. **Territorial Recognition:** ". . . dwelt in the land of Nod, on the east of Eden." General extent and boundaries are indicated with geographic notation. Fully-developed human characteristics are certainly in view with emphasis on recognition of those boundaries.

21. **Material Accumulation (Individual):** "And he builded a city. . . ." Accumulation beyond food gathering is a uniquely human experience. Structured city-building indicates sophistication.

22. **Cultural Identification:** "He builded a city, and called the name of the city. . . ." There is no mistaking the fact that cultural extension and establishment are intended in the text. Scope and extent are not indicated, but cultural implications are explicit.

23. **Engineering Development:** ". . . builded a city. . . ." In order to build or envision a city of any size or com-

plexity, conceptional engineering functions are necessary. In some undeveloped communities, these functions are not written or even expressed, but the functions are envisioned and employed. The ability to place one small building in relation to another is a basic concept requiring engineering perspective.

24. **Offspring Endowment:** ". . . and called the name of the city after the name of his son, Enoch." Filial endowments are recognized as being an "ultimate" resource and expression of *Homo sapiens.* To find this characteristic listed among the ancients invited a restructuring of our views on man's history.

25. **Material Accumulation (Cultural):** ". . . dwell in tents . . . have cattle. . . ." Enlarged numbers of individuals are emphasized in the context of having possessions. Previously an individual had built a city, and now the description reaches beyond incidental practice to include the community.

26. **Futuristic Projection:** "Jabal: he was the father of such as dwell in tents, and of such that have cattle." We here discover a principle of action and influence which intentionally passes to succeeding generations a resource of tents and cattle. Included in this influence upon future generations is the voluntary response of individuals within those future generations.

27. **Manual Dexterity:** ". . . such as handle the harp and the organ." Handling harps and organs requires conceptional and physical expertise of uncommon accomplishment. Skillful manipulation of instruments enlarges the musician and the cultural audience, particularly if the young are exposed to the influence of music.

28. **Artistic Appreciation:** *". . . all such as handle the harp and the organ."* A community or guild association is most definitely implicated within the statement. Responsive appreciation in harmony with skillful dexterity would warrant applause from any historian looking back on this generation.

29. **Responsibility Assumption:** *". . . an instructor of every artificer."* The text could imply that the instructor worked with every single individual who was learning to work as an artisan, or that he worked with individuals in various kinds of implements. In either case, the responsibility is phenomenal.

30. **Instructional Comprehension:** *". . . instructor of every. . . ."* Cultural anthropologists and archaeologists have occupied decades in documenting isolated cultures in an attempt to follow their growth patterns from implement fabrication to instructional repetition. When this facility is verified, the colony is identified as being industrialized. Such is the case in this text.

31. **Systematic Education:** *". . . instructor of every artificer in brass and iron."* If the intent of the text is that each succeeding student is referred to the primary instructor, or that artisans are returning to the primary instructor as they take on work with new materials, the result is the same: systematic instruction is established within a community or the entire culture.

32. **Technological Advancement:** *". . . in brass and iron."* Those who examine ancient civilizations separate brass and iron into distinct eras of development. Specific technology is required in the research (even if it is "trial and error") and repeatable methods of fabri-

cating implements from metallic bases. The purpose in making specific implements involved an advancement in the use of tools. Spanning both eras in the fabrication and purposeful use of the instrumentation demands a comprehension and assimilation at least equal to our own advanced civilization; and it probably deserves a designation superior to our own.

33. **Attire Awareness:** "And Lamech said unto his two wives, Adah and Zillah. . . ." In the original Hebrew the name *Adah* means "elegant ornament." Names are given designating a characteristic held by the person being named (or renamed), or a characteristic desired by the person giving the name. Such designations are given in reference to a known commodity or characteristic within the sphere of experience. Ornamentation and attire must have been observed in order to make such a distinction within the naming of an individual.

34. **Personal Defense:** "And Lamech said unto his two wives, Adah and Zillah, Hear my voice; ye wives of Lamech, Hearken unto my speech: for I have slain a man to my wounding, and a young man to my hurt. If Cain shall be avenged sevenfold, truly Lamech seventy and sevenfold." A marvelous explanation is here offered by a husband found slaying a young man who had wounded him and who had intended ultimate harm to him. Apparently desiring the good will and understanding of his wives, Lamech presented a full explanation on his own behalf. He was no longer in danger from the murderous young man, but he offers a self-defense explanation for his own home and perhaps in view of repercussions which might follow afterward.

35. **Comparative Justice:** "If Cain shall be avenged sevenfold, truly Lamech seventy and sevenfold." Reference is made to Cain, who in the past had sevenfold penalty promised upon anyone executing further injury toward him, and a "true" declaration of rightness is stated with a seventy and sevenfold vengeance.

36. **Judicial Consensus:** ". . . said unto his wives . . . hearken unto my speech. . . ." The speaker is asking both persons addressed to listen and follow with consent. Extensive detail is given with a specific request relating to those details. Reference is made by Lamech to his "speech." A deliberate attempt is made to gain a unified response from both persons addressed. This is strikingly similar to our own judicial system.

37. **Logistic Reasoning:** ". . . to my wounding . . . to my hurt . . . avenged sevenfold . . . truly seventy and sevenfold." Explanation is given twice that the young man was performing moral damage against the speaker. There is a progression of criminal infliction from "wounding" to ultimate "hurt" (death) being exercised by the offending party. An appeal is made to understand that the speaker had slain the young man in order to protect his own life. Then a reference to comparative vengeance is claimed. This included both inductive and deductive reasoning powers in brilliant display.

38. **Speech Declamation:** "Hearken unto my speech. . . ." What follows is based on reflection, is thought out in advance, is addressed to a given audience, is systematic in presenting details, and is specific in requesting a response. This we call speech form, and it represents complicated actions, reasoning powers, and delivery.

39. **Peer Relationship:** "Hearken. . . ." Relationship both in the present and in the response rendered in the future are encompassed in the related text. Sympathetic understanding is obviously requested by Lamech.

40. **Reputation Status:** ". . . I have slain a man. . . ." This context clearly bears the sense of Lamech's concern for understanding among those who would learn of the event. Great pains are taken to explain that the young man was attempting to slay the speaker.

41. **Emotional Response (Positive):** "And Adam knew his wife again; and she bore a son, and called his name Seth: For God, said she, hath appointed me another seed instead of Abel, whom Cain slew." A child is named in grateful response to a loving God who understood the emotional void left after a previous child had been lost. Civilized awareness and conscientious response ensue.

42. **Providential Compensation:** ". . . hath appointed me another seed instead of Abel, whom Cain slew." Awareness of providential justice and purpose underlies a basic philosophy within a culture. Ancient ability to hold a concept of benevolent philosophy endows ancient man with extremely sophisticated thought processes. In some instances, man is able to purposefully and benevolently display consideration upon another. To no less a degree his awareness of divine intervention for his benefit would reflect the existence of this major sophisticated characteristic within ancient man.

43. **Historical Perspective:** "And Adam lived an hundred and thirty years, and begat a son in his own likeness." A sense of having counted each year with its relation-

ship in time to preceding and succeeding years is complicated enough, especially without ancestors to give a learning reference. In this instance, we have exposed an additional ability—that of recycling number values, i.e., counting past one hundred. Additionally, we have related the birth of a son, and the son is associated with and compared to the characteristics of his father. Passage of time and events with association are in view.

44. **Obituarial Documentation:** "And Adam lived . . . begat sons and daughters . . . and he died." Only advanced peoples record the births, events, offspring, and death of inhabitants. This practice memorializes the memory and record for succeeding generations.

45. **Religious Influence:** "And he called his name Enos, then began men to call on the name of the Lord." A very interesting enlightenment is here provided for anthropologists, in keeping with their observations in numerous cultures. The child is named Enos, which means, "a living moral individual" (and one who by definition is obligated to be appreciative to the One who gave him life, and one who is dependent on his Creator for sustaining that life). His name takes the form of a declared statement. The influence of that name is that men "begin to call upon the name of the Lord." The meaning and person of the name influenced men in religious response to call upon the Name of the Creator who is needed to sustain all men as mortals. This humble religious response is anthropologically elevating, because "primitive" cultures tend to think of themselves as "the only people," rather than responding in religious humility.

46. **Genetic Superiority:** "And Adam [and Eve] were an hundred and thirty years old, and begat a son. . . ." The ability to conceive and birth a son at one hundred thirty, then to continue to bear sons and daughters is indicative of superior genetics. Purpose in the genetic design is demonstrated as each reproduces after its kind.

47. **Genetic Viability:** ". . . begat sons and daughters . . . dwelt in tents . . . instructed . . . handled . . . hearken . . . built. . . ." Dimensional and resourcefully reflective existence is portrayed among these ancients. They are seen as being at home in their environment, and in the truest anthropological sense, affecting that environment.

48. **Origins Inquisition:** "And he called his name Noah, saying, This same shall comfort us concerning our work and toil of our hands, because of the ground which the Lord hath cursed." The basic philosophic inquiries are: Who am I? Where did I come from? What is my purpose here? Where am I going? To find reference to these inquiries as a unit given in one succinct record among ancient peoples is most enlightening. The "who" ("us") is emphasized in relation to the "purpose" ("toil and work of our hands"—burdensome labor balanced with meaningful accomplishment), and the "where am I going" ("comfort"— hope for the future) is given in the same sentence with the "where did I come from" (from a history of "toil" physically and a relationship of accountability to the "Lord, my Creator" physiologically).

49. **Individual Achievement:** ". . . mighty men which were of old, men of renown." Numbers of legendary ac-

complishments are ascribed to a number of individual men. Renowned among their peers, the ancient achievers are catalogued in the record.

50. **Recording Capability**: ". . . the same became . . . men of renown." The list included more than the accomplishments of a single man; it refers to men considered mighty and who were renowned within their own lifetimes. Whether the record of their deeds was oral or written is immaterial. To have mentally recorded names, ages, births, deaths, and accomplishments is as astonishing an accomplishment as developing a system of writing.

51. **Inventive Precognition**: ". . . imagination of the thoughts of his heart." Precognition is defined as the ability to think beforehand or to mentally design in advance. The emphasis within the text is that of proliferating deeds as a result of imaginative capacities. This ability can only be equated with our most advanced leaders, scientists, and researchers in today's academic institutions.

52. **Directed Concentration**: ". . . great in the earth . . . every imagination . . . only . . . continually." Performance of deeds resulted from concerted mental activity. A unified purpose aligned with a very active motivated imagination characterized the entire culture and was practiced individually throughout the society. To find a record of this unified practice among all citizens strongly suggests that the gene pool was superior, recent, and uncontaminated.

53. **Criminal Propensity (Cultural)**: ". . . wickedness of man was great in the earth . . . every imagination . . . only evil continually." The best modern illustration

corresponding to this extensive social disease is that of Nazi Germany under Hitler. Negative vices require as much mental ingenuity as do positive virtues.

54. **Purposeful Motivation (Negative):** "The earth was also corrupt . . . filled with violence." Individual incessant action was applied which violated established moral values (the term "corrupt" was used).

55. **Social Influence:** "All flesh had corrupted his way." Anthropologists make notations for the seemingly incidental behavior of all members of a clan, tribe, or culture. It is recognized that this seemingly incidental activity is inherently bound to the total genetic potential of the group as a whole. The whole culture was impressionable to the point of responding to the synergistic influence of violent corruption.

56. **Purposeful Motivation (Positive):** "Thus did Noah; according to all that God commanded him, so did he." Emphasis is placed on the words "all . . . commanded . . . did." That one man (and his family) had the physical, mental, and volitional capacity to follow purposeful instruction with conscious extended performance, and that the rest of an entire race of man was purposefully motivated to violate the same expressed instruction, emphasizes very strong evidence that the race as a whole possessed the genetic capabilities of each member of the race.

We listed fifty-six superior characteristics pre-flood man possessed. These characteristics to some degree would have been related to the early generations after the biblical Noahic flood, because man was superior in his genetic characteristics, and thus was able to transmit and receive many of these characteristics without the benefit of a written record.

Written records are observable for us, however. For example, a very special bit of data had not been highly publicized, but has certainly been researched and verified. In the area of Cro-Magnon man, or Magdalenian-period Stone Age man, a very high sophistication capability has been evidenced, not only in his ability to draw in the caves, but also in a documented bit of evidence which verifies the concept of the orchestral creation model. This concept supports the notion that ancient man was a sophisticated man, and by ancient man we are not far removed in time from him, not nearly as far as the evolutionists would suppose.

Rene Noorbergen relates the following evidence in his classic work:

> In a cave near Lussac-les-Cateaux, in 1937, Leon Pericard and Stephane Lwoff uncovered a number of engraved stones dating from the Magdalenian period which drastically altered the accepted picture. The flat stones showed men and women in casual poses, wearing robes, boots, belts, coats, and hats. One engraving is a profile of a young lady who appears to be sitting and watching something. She is dressed in a pant suit with a short-sleeved jacket, a pair of small boots, and a decorated hat that flops down over her right ear and touches her shoulder. Resting on her lap is a square, flat object that folds down the front, very much like a modern purse. Other examples show men wearing well-tailored pants and coats, broad belts with clasps, and clipped beards and moustaches.

. . . The Lussac models are by no means the only evidence of a sophisticated dress from the Stone Age. Prehistoric cave printings from the Kalahari Desert of Southwest Africa, dated within the Stone Age period, show light-skinned men with blond beards and well-styled hair, wearing boots, tight-fitting pants, multi-colored shirts, and coats and gloves.

Such accounts of the earliest history of man do not indicate that he was a brute beast. In fact, the opposite is true. Man, when he appeared on the Earth, was very sophisticated. Given the context in which man was living at the time, and driven by circumstances, whether temporary or semipermanent, man's behavior and lifestyle were compatible with today's contemporary society.

Anthropological and historical records show that man has from time to time lived in caves. The Nabateans, an advanced and resourceful people, lived almost entirely in caves in the Petra area of southern Jordan. There are areas in the world today where the environmental factors still make cave dwelling preferable.

The fact that man was able to display superior characteristics at the very beginning of his existence, a composite picture of intelligent and compassionate human being, shows that man had to be created. He could not have evolved. Man possessed superior characteristics and arrived on the scene fully mature. This evident truth supports the concept of orchestrated creation.

Diagram D: RESTRUCTURE OF MAN'S DESCENT

EVOLUTIONARY CONCEPT: CREATION CONCEPT:

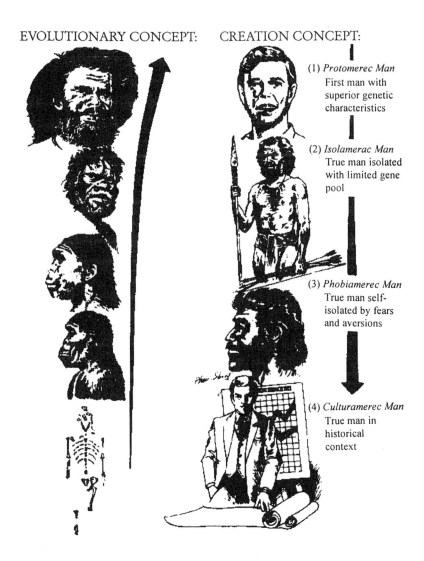

(1) *Protomerec Man*
First man with
superior genetic
characteristics

(2) *Isolamerac Man*
True man isolated
with limited gene
pool

(3) *Phobiamerec Man*
True man self-
isolated by fears
and aversions

(4) *Culturamerec Man*
True man in
historical
context

Chapter Four

Firmament Around
the Earth

In the course of our discussions, we will observe some of the details of the pre-flood world. We will examine what effect the great flood had on that environment, and we will project that world prophetically to the restored Earth. We will observe from the biblical record and from correlated scientific research a possible mechanism for re-establishing the firmament canopy during the restored Earth.

As this author has lectured across the United States, and internationally as well, I have found a greater response in this area of study than in any other of scientific creationism. Let us now consider what the pre-flood world was like.

Imagine a scale model of what the Earth would look like if it were cut in half. A good comparison would be an apple cut in half, for the Earth is not a perfect sphere, and there is a dip in the electromagnetic field. That dip needs to be portrayed in that schematic design.

Genesis 1 states:

> In the beginning God created the heaven and the earth. And the earth was without form, and void; and darkness was upon the face of the deep. And the spirit of God moved upon the face of the waters.

These verses show that even on the first day of creation, before God created light, God created the Earth in a watery form. This is extremely important.

Studies done by renowned physicists, such as Dr. Russell Humphreys, show that each molecule of water possesses a small electromagnetic field. When these molecules are aligned, the result is a composite electromagnetic charge of all the molecules of water that are aligned. When all of these molecules are in composite alignment, you have the composite energy of all of the molecules.

God began by creating the Earth first in all the universe, even before creating the electromagnetic spectrum of light into the heavenly bodies, such as the sun and the stellar heavens. God has a very special purpose for Earth, which is described throughout the Word of God. On Earth, it was God's design to create man in His own image. After the fall of man, it was Earth that received very specialized attention from God. God's Son, some four thousand years later, came to live on Earth, and to give His life as a ransom. It was on Earth that Jesus Christ shed His blood. It was on Earth that death was defeated. It was on Earth that the resurrection took place. The Creator God, in the form of the second person Jesus Christ, experienced death and was raised back to life by His own power and the power of the Holy Spirit. It was on Earth that God exercised His will, even by permitting evil and destruction by giving man a moral choice.

It will be on Earth that the final drama of satanic defeat will be played out. It will be on Earth that Christ will return and exercise His power by ruling and reigning for a thousand literal years. It will be on Earth that a visible glimpse of the celestial city will eternally be seen, for Heaven will orbit above the Earth in perpetual, everlasting form. In Galatians 4:4–5, we are told:

> . . . God sent forth his Son, made of a woman, made under the law, To redeem them that were under the law, that we might receive the adoption of sons.

All this took place on Earth. Earth is very important.

We believe we have some indication as to why God first created the Earth as a sphere of water. *God has the answer before we have the problem.* The life forms that God would create on day number three, being in botanical form, would require this water. On day number five, God would design the fish and fowl. Each of these creatures would require this water. On day number six, God would create insects, dinosaurs, man, and woman before the day was finished. It is not like God to cause His creation to stand in want. God has the answer in the form of water, before we have the problem of needing it.

We also believe that God began by creating the Earth as a sphere of water because *water is a type of the Word of God.* We are refreshed by the Word of God. It is this revelation in the biblical record that gives us a clear, unfolding, dimensional perspective of what God did with this void, formless composite of water called the Earth. We know what God did with that composite of water because it is revealed in the Word of God. We need the biblical record for a clear understanding of what He did with the Earth and the days in which He made certain particular details evident.

Water is a type of the Holy Spirit. We need the Holy Spirit to guide us through the pages of the Bible. God used the Holy Spirit, and the Holy Spirit was very active in the entire creation of the whole orchestral plan. While Jesus Christ, the second Person of the Trinity, was the primary agent in creation, God the Father and God the Holy Spirit were certainly active during the creation as well.

Water is a type of personal salvation. Having a perfectly designed and orchestrated Earth and universe, with a perfectly created and companioned man, is not enough. Man needs fellowship with his Creator. Water is a type of salvation in Christ Jesus. We need that personal relationship with our Creator.

Water is a type of the person of Jesus Christ. Jesus said: "I am the Way. I am the Truth. I am the Life. I am the Water. I am the Door." He is all of those things, and He is the water of life. Jesus told the Samaritan woman at the well in John 4:14:

> But whosoever drinketh of the water that I shall give him shall never thirst; but the water that I shall give him shall be in him a well of water springing up into everlasting life.

Jesus Christ is typified by water, and orchestrated creation makes evident the design of Jesus Christ.

On day number three God would create the other elements in perfect balance. He created the botanical life forms, full-bloomed, with the seeds within the life form. On day number two, however, God did a very special thing. It is obvious from the context that God used the elements of water—that is, hydrogen and oxygen—to create the firmament. In Genesis 1:6-8, we have a marvelous statement. It is simple on the surface, but marvelous in its consequences.

> And God said, Let there be a firmament in the midst of the waters, and let it divide the waters from the waters. And God made the firmament, and divided the waters which were under the firmament from the waters which were above the firmament: and it was so. And God called the firmament Heaven. And the evening and the morning were the second day.

It is obvious from the biblical context that this firmament included two composite layers of water, adjacent on each side with a firmament in the middle. Some biblical exegetes have suggested that perhaps this firmament referred to the expanse, and the water on the surface of the Earth was in one composite form. They also maintain that we had a bubble of water approximately eleven miles above the Earth as a second layer. However, the clear scriptural mandate is that this entire firmament was encased by layers of water on both sides as a composite part of the firmament. Later, the Scripture describes the seas and oceans on the surface of the Earth.

We can, therefore, envision a model of the firmament

approximately eleven miles above the surface of the Earth. We believe the firmament was approximately eleven miles above the surface because there exists a heat sink at that elevation. Nearer to the Earth it is warmer for at least some space. If we were to amass the amounts of water present on Earth, and assimilate the greater amount of water within the Earth, this would leave the approximate remainder of a few inches thick lineal dimension double encasement of water in solid crystalline form as the firmament.

This is extremely important. Here we have a firmament, not just water in cloud or vaporous form, but in solid form. The Hebrew context shows that the water and the firmament are in a very special form. It was apparently in crystalline form—pure, transparent, relatively thin ice. It was probably no more than twenty feet thick at best. The Hebrew word used to describe this firmament is really quite astounding. In fact, if we do not follow the Hebrew literally, our model does not work at all. The biblical record has to be literal, or it really isn't verifiable. This firmament had to be of literal composite, just as the Scripture stated.

The word used in the Hebrew to describe the firmament is *raqia*. Hebrew scholars recognize that the word *raqia* means to compress or pound out, and stretch out this arch of heaven in thin metal sheets. However, the elements used in the firmament are the elements of water. It was not until day number three that God created the rest of the elements.

On day number one, God concluded the creation of the day by saying: "It is good." On days three through six, He also concluded the days' creations by saying: "It is good." However, on day number two, God did not say that it was good. This does not mean that it wasn't. It simply means that on day number one, He had already pronounced it as good. If God says anything in a singular dimension, it applies to all. He had already said it was good. He did not create new elements on day number two; He simply used the elements He created on day number one—the elements of hydrogen and oxygen.

Many very fine scientific creation researchers have envisioned for decades that there was a greenhouse effect before the flood, and in all probability there was. They envisioned that there was water vapor, perhaps in cloud form, above the Earth. However, if we simply use the vaporous form of water, the scriptural mandate in Genesis 1:14–18 cannot be fulfilled, because it says the stars were "set" or enhanced—added in full dimension to this firmament. If the firmament cover had simply been water vapor, the stars would only have been seen in approximately eighty percent of the detail that we see today. Yet the biblical record says that they were enhanced. The original Hebrew word used is the word *nathan*. The literal translation means that they were added and yielded in full dimension within this firmament. The only way this could have worked is for the word *raqia* to have a literal meaning.

Researcher Dan Cook spoke to one of the physicists involved in the hydrogen bomb project at Laurence Livermore National Laboratories. That physicist related to him that scientists there, some years back, took the elements of water and compressed them under super cold, cryogenic circumstances. Hydrogen became near-metallic in form, and took on the characteristics of metal. It became crystalline, transparent, fiber optic, superconductive, and ferromagnetic. All of these characteristics have tremendous implications.

The hydrogen in the water was compressed and energized, and the pressure held in stasis form because of the crystalline ice on each side, for the biblical record states that God made the firmament in the middle, with water above and water beneath. Under such super cold circumstances where great pressure exists, in addition to tremendous energy, hydrogen takes on metallic characteristics. Envision the Earth before the flood, with a firmament consisting of compressed energized hydrogen taking on near-metallic characteristics, in the middle of a solid water formation suspended about eleven miles above the Earth. This configuration would have done some wonderful things.

On day number four, when the sun was created, the energy of the sun upon this hydrogen would have caused a gentle pink glow. At high noon there would have been a light pink coloration in the sky; at sunrise and sunset there would have been a vivid pink coloration; and at midnight there would have been a magenta pink sky. In other words, the sky before the flood was never totally dark.

The biblical record states that God made the greater light to rule the day, and the lesser light to rule the night. We have assumed for centuries that the greater light was the sun and the lesser light was the moon. The moon certainly bears an impact on and, to some degree, affects the Earth. However, the moon does not always remain in visual form. The lesser light ruling the night, consequently, was not only the moon, even though the moon certainly has a purpose in the orchestrated model. The lesser light ruling the night included transfer of energy from the day side of the Earth along the lines of this *raqia* firmament. The electromagnetic energy was carried along the elemental lines of near-metallic hydrogen, which was fiber optic in nature. This would cause a twilight glow on the night side of the Earth, while on the day side of the Earth the greater light would literally rule the day.

The statement is made that this light "ruled the day." Scientists and researchers are finding that the most important color in the spectrum is pink. This is the color that is produced by energized hydrogen. They find that plants grow better under pink light and that individuals respond more positively in mood to pink light. Researchers have found that when a person is affected by the right spectrum of pink light, the brain secretes norepinephren. Norepinephren is a natural tranquilizer and neurotransmitter. Before the flood, man was dominated by various spectra of pink light. The tranquillity of his environment offered him the ability to have his brain work at maximum efficiency. The firmament made that possible with a gentle pink glow in various spectral forms, with the greater light ruling the day and the lesser light ruling the night. God made a wonderful orchestral creation, and man ultimately received the full benefit.

Diagram A: ORCHESTRAL CREATION MODEL

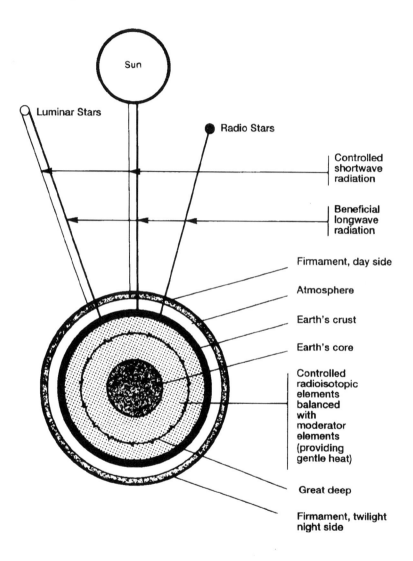

Sun

Luminar Stars

Radio Stars

Controlled shortwave radiation

Beneficial longwave radiation

Firmament, day side

Atmosphere

Earth's crust

Earth's core

Controlled radioisotopic elements balanced with moderator elements (providing gentle heat)

Great deep

Firmament, twilight night side

Chapter Five

Optimal Pressure and
Pink Light

In the previous chapter, I shared with you some of the physical characteristics of the world before the flood. We referred particularly to the firmament, or canopy, which was suspended approximately eleven miles above the Earth in Noah's day. This firmament consisted of a layer of water, probably between ten and twenty feet thick, and it extended completely around the Earth.

There are records, archaeologically discerned, among many cultures which refer to a time in the past when the sky "hung low." The biblical record, however, gives a far better explanation: firmament.

As we have already noted, this canopy could not possibly have simply been a cloud cover or water vapor. Unless we carefully follow the environmental description in the Bible, the purpose the firmament served would make no sense.

As we also noted in the previous chapter, in doing

research on the hydrogen bomb, physicists at Lawrence Livermore National Laboratories took the element of hydrogen (an element of water) and compressed it under super cold temperatures. When the pressure reached a certain degree under diamond points, the hydrogen took on near-metallic characteristics: superconductive, transparent, fiber optic, ferromagnetic, and crystalline in form. This is astounding because the biblical record states that God made the firmament on the second day of creation. The Hebrew word for firmament is *raqia*, which means to press, or pound together into thin metal sheets. This is the explanation of how the canopy, or arch of heaven, was formed and stretched out around the world in thin metal sheets. The metallic description of the firmament given in Genesis puzzled us for many years in our scientific creation research. But when we learned to simply take the biblical account literally, as God intended, we discovered that one of the elements in water (hydrogen) binds together in a crystalline lattice. Under such pressurized transformation, the hydrogen in water takes on the characteristics as described in the biblical account of creation.

We are informed in Genesis 1:16 that the greater light was to rule the day and the lesser light was to rule the night. The transfer of light, fiber optically, means that the greater penetration of light during the day would produce varying shades of pink, and the lesser light of night would produce a deeper shade of pink, in addition to an enhanced moon.

Biologists have found that the greatest plant growth is encouraged under pink light. Further investigation has revealed that it is pink light which optimally triggers the growth of cells within plants. It is no wonder that within the fossil record we find such things as giant mosses called the Lepidodendrons. The modern variation is the Lycopsid club moss that grows to an approximate maximum height of sixteen inches. But in fossil records, the same variety of moss grew to be over one hundred feet tall. A contributing factor to the enormous size of plant life before the flood was energized hydrogen in the firmament giving off the pinkish glow.

The enormous size of plant life in the Antediluvian world also dictated the size of certain forms of animal life, or dinosaurs. On day number six, the final animal life was created, and in order to keep the vegetation in balance, such huge plant-eating creatures were required. After the flood, the decline in the size and abundance of plant life would not have supported the dinosaurs for very long. Even elephants today in Africa are threatened by the lack of needed vegetation to support them. Reduced partial pressure in the atmosphere played an even greater role in the demise of the dinosaur.

In the world before the flood, the light would be at its lowest pink hue at high noon because of the angle of the light passing through the firmament. But, just as important, envision the firmament—this double bubble of crystalline water—and the effect it would have upon the atmospheric pressure. The atmosphere would be pressurized to a greater degree than we now have. Researchers like Dr. Henry Voss at the University of Illinois, have been able to approximate the atomic weight of such a canopy. This crystalline canopy would put a cap on the atmosphere. Atmospheric pressure today at sea level is 14.7 pounds per square inch. Before the flood, the air pressure would have been about two times what it is today.

Obviously, the heavier air pressure before the flood would have had a greater effect on plant and animal life than it does today. The ratio of oxygen in the atmosphere would have been about thirty percent, compared to twenty-one percent today. Some researchers have concluded that due to the pre-flood atmospheric conditions which had greater amounts of oxygen, man could have run up to two hundred miles without suffering fatigue. It has been discovered in hyperbaric medical chamber experiments that under these circumstances an open wound would heal overnight. It is therefore understandable how man could have lived to be several hundred years old, even after the fall, in this pre-flood world. Heavier air pressure and more oxygen in the atmosphere were conducive to longer life.

Another factor in the pre-flood environment which was in man's favor was less radiation from the sun. The canopy above the Earth acted as a filter to trap most of the shortwave radiation. It is the shortwave radiation that is causing man many problems today. Ultraviolet radiation is streaming down at an alarming rate. The Environmental Protection Agency has announced that in a matter of decades, one out of every three persons will die of cancer due to increased ultraviolet radiation. But before the flood, almost all of the harmful radiation would have been filtered out by the water canopy.

Today, because of harmful shortwave radiation, man suffers genetic damage, cancer, and other health damage factors that shorten the lifespan. Also, there are certain microbes and disease germs that could not live in the pre-flood atmosphere, but they can live in an oxygen-depleted atmosphere. In addition, there was a mist each morning that aided the oxygenation of the entire water table. More oxygen in the water would account for great whales, great sharks, and the chambered nautilus marine life forms that were gargantuan in size. The fossil record bears evidence that such creatures existed, but without more oxygen in the waters today, they could not live in contemporary oceans, seas, or rivers. The theory of evolution does not provide an answer as to how such enormous marine monsters lived, but the creation model does provide an answer.

Before the flood, man was encased in a perfect environment. The water table, being energized, fostered an abundance of fish and marine life of every size and description. The filtering of ultraviolet radiation would permit plant life to grow in abundance and to enormous proportions. An additional beneficial characteristic would be the extra oxygen in the atmosphere, and with the great assimilation of oxygen in the air, man was possibly twenty percent larger than he is today. Adam and Noah were probably about seven feet tall, and there were others who were even taller.

In the sixth chapter of Genesis, we read that there were giants on the Earth before the flood. At Glen Rose, Texas, we have excavated some of the footprints of those giants. Their footprints were preserved as they walked over the muddy sediment in the early phases of the Noahic flood.

The environmental context before the flood would exercise the full genetic viability for all life forms. For example, today the dragonfly—which is a superior helicopter—has a wingspan not exceeding six inches. But in the fossil record, dragonflies have been found with wingspans of up to thirty-six inches. There has to be an explanation as to how at some point in time dragonflies grew to such gigantic dimensions. It would certainly require a greater concentration of oxygen. Conditions that would support such monstrous life forms, even in the insect world, scientifically dictate that there had to be such a canopy above the Earth. In order to provide that much oxygen for animal life forms which were several times larger than are in evidence today, the oxygen would have to approach the level of toxicity, unless the atmospheric pressure was greater. Again, such an atmospheric condition can only be explained in terms of a firmament. Therefore, we have to follow the biblical record of creation specifically or the environmental chain breaks into unconnected parts.

The greater atmospheric pressure, with approximately thirty percent oxygen, would have created optimal conditions. Thus, dragonflies could have grown to a size supporting a thirty-six inch wingspan.

Consider another illustration. In west Texas, there has been found a fossilized pterodactyl, a flying reptile, with a wingspan of fifty-two feet. There is no way this flying dinosaur (as it has been called) could have flown with the current atmospheric pressure. It would have been utterly impossible. But, with an atmospheric pressure of approximately thirty-two pounds per square inch, this flying pterodactyl would have had a field day.

Scientific investigation mandates a time in the past when life forms required greater atmospheric pressure and filtration of the ultraviolet radiation, such as the biblical record very clearly presents. In all the annals of investigative research, only the biblical record gives the required mechanism to make this possible. Just a canopy or water vapor would not satisfy a complete and needed explanation. Water vapor collapses into vortices, eddies, and spiral circles of energy, but with a world energized by a firmament of compressed hydrogen held in place by a layer of crystalline water which would keep the temperature at a consistent level, the necessary requirements would be the result.

NASA had discovered in the examination of superconductive materials that when held near a magnet, the lines of force generated in the free flow of electromagnetic energy hold the materials in place, either above it or below it. In other words, researchers have not been able to find a mechanism for holding up a canopy unless that water canopy has exactly what the biblical record clearly describes: a superconductive solid metallic base. Hydrogen would be such a base under these circumstances, and with a free flow of electrons, it would support itself above the dipole magnet of the Earth. All the laws of physics known in current research show that this would simply support itself above the Earth, and it would be held there until warmer temperatures would moderate its enclosure, as we will discuss later.

In capsulization, the environmental evidence of the pre-flood world indicated it was like this: A superconductive canopy of compressed hydrogen in near-metallic form was encased above and below in crystalline water. The stars were shining at a distance, a startling characteristic of the pre-flood world. In Genesis 1:14–18, the stellar heavens are described. The stars are in color, and the biblical record states that God set the stars in the firmament. The ancients described the firmament as a vault above the Earth, and the stars were placed in this vault. This is not what the biblical record says to us. The biblical record states very clearly that God "set" the stars in the firmament much as a jeweler would enhance a diamond by placing it on a background of black velvet. The word "set" is taken from the Hebrew word *nathan*; it means "to add and yield." In other words, the stars are not physically placed in the firmament, because they are great distances away. But, as light from the stars penetrate the firmament, there is a very strong magnetic field in the middle; it is superconductive without any resistance to the flow of electrons. On each side is an electromagnetic field charged to a lesser degree in the crystalline water formation. What is then presented in a pressurized form on each side is a photo-multiplier. Each photon of light which strikes the configuration is multiplied by ten because of the interaction in the atoms. On the Earth side of the canopy, the stars were seen with ten times the photons that the light brought to the outer surface of the canopy. Before the flood, the stars were seen by man as being about three times brighter than they are seen today. In other words, in the firmament, God set the stars, or added and yielded their dimensions in full color.

NASA has found that when a red filter is used in space, the stars appear in beautiful color. This is exciting because God put the stellar bodies in space for signs, for days, for months, and for years. We understand that by observing the rotation of the Earth in relation to the movement of the sun and the moon, and other heavenly bodies, we can tell time. But now we can perceive that with the enhancement of the light, those before the flood could, by the configuration of the stars, tell time at any moment. They would not need a Rolex watch; they would have something far better.

Before the flood, Earth's inhabitants never saw total darkness. Research has indicated that the temperature would have been about seventy-two degrees Fahrenheit at night, and about seventy-eight degrees Fahrenheit during the day. Imagine superior man with a perfect environment, perfect food with complete nutrients, no harmful radiation from space, and disease microbes held in check. The pre-flood world was, in our understanding today, paradise.

The orchestral creation model proves that there was a Designer, and that all of His design met the needs of a special creature made in His image, the creature we call man.

Chapter Six

Music in the Stars and
Design in the Earth

In this chapter, let us examine some exciting details in this orchestral creation model. In the book of Job, God gave a discourse to Job that we have only now been able to understand to any great degree. In this chapter, God asked the question: "Where wast thou . . . When the morning stars sang together, and all the sons of God shouted for joy?" (Job 38:4, 7).

This author publicly spoke on this passage for decades. However, a few months ago, when examining the original Hebrew text of this passage, I discovered that God was not only speaking of the morning stars "singing" during the first week of creation, but of this being a continuing context, from Adam all the way through Noah, and continuing to the present day. According to the observation of radioastrophysicists, stars, by radio wave context, are "singing" to us.

NASA discovered some years ago that not only are

the stars giving off radio waves, but some of the stars are giving off one million times as much radio energy as is produced in our entire Milky Way Galaxy. Stars throughout the universe are emitting radio wave energy. Some entire galaxies are emitting almost nothing but radio wave energy. NASA discovered to their amazement that not only are these stars emitting radio waves of energy, but that there is music on those radio waves of energy. NASA also discovered that not only is music emitted, but the music being emitted is in a major key. The music being emitted from these stars is harmonious. NASA compared the music being emitted from these star sources to the instruments of an orchestra that are all in tune with each other.

This evidence seems to verify the existence of an orchestral creation. It seems that everywhere we look, creation is orchestrated. Recently, with some special plasma ionized research units, NASA found that Neptune and some of the other planets in our solar system emit a signal which sounds like whistling, as if it were whistling a tune.

According to the thirty-eighth chapter of Job, before the flood not only did the morning stars sing together, but the sons of God shouted for joy. They were required by the nature of what was within man to respond enthusiastically. How was this possible?

Let's take into consideration the information that has been presented so far. First of all, there was a firmament of water above the Earth in crystalline form. Crystals take on very special characteristics. When energized with a current of electromagnetic energy, crystals amplify long radio waves. Each morning before the flood, as the Earth turned into the sunlight, and the angle was just right, the energized radio waves reaching Earth through the universe were amplified by the crystalline firmament canopy. Each morning before the flood the radio wave signals from these stars, or "music," could be heard on Earth.

Light energy does something to the human body and to all life forms, even if it cannot be seen. In the early hours of the morning, as the fiber optic nature of this crystalline canopy above the Earth was transferring light from the sunny side of the globe, it would have very gently enhanced that light. If an individual were asleep, and could not see the light, as the light was enhanced that individual would begin to stir, for the light would be received in the biologic mechanism of his body. Light would gently induce the individual to awaken.

The crystalline water in the firmament canopy before the flood would filter out the harmful shortwave radiation. The canopy would permit the long waves of energy to go right through it. In fact, long waves of energy would not only be able to pass through the canopy, but would be enhanced, or amplified, by it. While the individual sleeping before the flood was gently induced to awaken by the light, about dawn he would also have been greeted by the amplified sound of the radio wave energy being emitted by the stars.

NASA had found that there are bursts of energy from these sources. Not only would there be individual sound frequencies from these far star sources, but there would also be sustains, crescendos, diminishes, and terminations. There would be new music every day.

In the orchestral creation model as described in part in Job 38, God said there were foundations to the Earth, and that there were elements in perfect balance. Inside the Earth there existed the radioisotopes in perfect balance with moderators, such as iridium, strontium, rubidium, radioisotopic lead, and uranium, in perfect balance with manganese, water, sulfur, magnesium, and other elemental moderators. Under those circumstances, inside the Earth there would have existed a perfectly controlled nuclear reaction. Not only would there have been a nuclear reactor, but with the elements placed in perfect balance, there would have been what physicists now call a breeder reactor. You would have ended up with as many elements as you started with, as long as there was a constant energy input into the system. The constant energy input was generated throughout the celestial heavens and received into the crystalline firmament canopy, and the primary electromagnetic field of the canopy transferred this energy to the secondary electromagnetic field of the dipole magnet of the Earth. Thus, the energy supply would have been continuously restructured and replaced. Under those circumstances, with the radioisotopes inside the Earth in a long-term decay rate, there would have existed a perfectly balanced nuclear reactor inside the Earth.

You would need such a perfectly balanced reactor in the orchestral model. It is primarily the shortwave energy which heats up the atmosphere around us every day. However, that shortwave energy would have been filtered out by the firmament canopy before the flood. The heating of the environment did not come from above. Instead, there would have been a gentle thermal blanket within the Earth, probably surrounded by a layer of asphalt inside the Earth called the "swaddlingband" in Job 38:9. This would moderate and sustain the temperature which would then be radiated to the Earth's surface. Possibly it would be returned to the surface of the Earth through water fountains and recycling reservoirs. This energy would be returned to the Earth so that at night the energy transferred into the Earth would cause the environment to be slightly cooler. During the daytime, because of this perfectly balanced thermonuclear reaction inside the Earth, it would have heated up slightly, to approximately seventy-eight degrees Fahrenheit.

With Job 38 as context, and with all of the natural elements in perfect balance, let us emphasize the element that is the most common worldwide. This element is silicon, or sand. Inside the Earth there would have existed a perfectly balanced nuclear reactor designed with radio-isotopes and moderators. Above that rested a solid crust of granite around the Earth, then above that there would have existed a layer of sand or silicon. Above this silicon layer would have been the vegetation. This configuration would have given a perfect hydroponic system in the water table for the plant growth. This would also have given a slightly warmer ambient temperature context for the root systems. Amazingly, botanists have found that when plants are grown hydroponically, they grow to be superior plants. When a plant is grown under pink light, it is superior. When the roots are slightly warmed, the plant grows and produces in a superior fashion. When the amount of carbon dioxide is slightly increased, the plant grows better still.

A Japanese physicist, Dr. Kei Mori, took only two of these gradient elements (he filtered the ultraviolet rays and increased the carbon dioxide) and exposed plant life to these conditions. In two years, under his supervision, a tomato plant grew to be sixteen feet tall with nine hundred and three tomatoes on it. The tomato plant has continued to grow to this day. Our last report shows that it is over five years old, over twenty feet tall, and has produced over four thousand tomatoes. All Dr. Mori did was filter out the ultraviolet rays and allow the plant to take in more carbon dioxide.

The United States Department of Agriculture simply added some carbon dioxide to cotton plants, and they found that it resulted in a thirty to fifty percent increase in growth rate. Before the flood, however, the following conditions existed that would have helped plants to grow better.

1. There existed increased atmospheric pressure.
2. Carbon dioxide was increased to an efficient degree.
3 Hydroponic growing conditions existed in which plant roots penetrated into the water table in the sand, thus the nutrients were better supplied.
4. There was a variation of flow within the water table.
5. There was a slightly warmer temperature gradient in the root systems and the water table.
6. There was efficient use of pink light.
7. There was an elimination of ultraviolet radiation.

No wonder such lush vegetation existed before the flood. Only scientific creation can, in principle, match the context that we find in the fossil record.

With the model that has been illustrated, since sand is also crystalline in structure, it is possible that the sand would be able to pick up and amplify with wonderful sounds the radio wave energy surrounding an individual. As we learn later in this book, the description of the restored Earth found in Isaiah 35 shows that the forests will again sing.

Around an individual before the flood in this canopy context, the radio waves from the stars were enhanced by this canopy in the morning hours. The crystalline structure of the sand would pick up and amplify these radio waves. Finally, there are qualities in the cellular structures of plants which would cause the reeds to vibrate, so the forest began to sing. Anyone who knew his Creator could not help but respond.

That is the reason God asked Job: "Where wast thou . . . When the morning stars sang together, and all the sons of God shouted for joy?" Everyone who was alive before the flood and knew the Lord, had to respond and sing along with the total environment. It surely must have been a Utopian world—an orchestrated world. Only now have we been able to put together this orchestral creation model, balancing out all of these elements in an articulated form. The biblical records explain reality far better than the evolutionary concept does. The facts that we find about us in nature and in the biblical account of creation invite us to know our Creator in the person of His Son, Jesus Christ.

Diagram B: MUSIC IN THE STARS

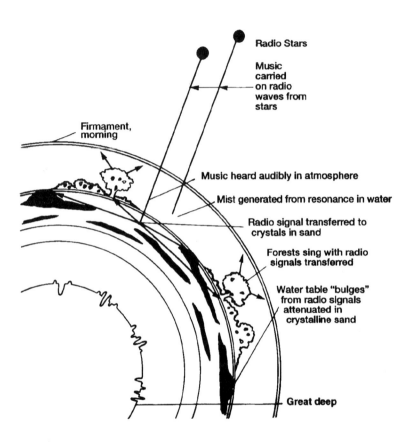

Radio Stars

Music carried on radio waves from stars

Music heard audibly in atmosphere

Mist generated from resonance in water

Radio signal transferred to crystals in sand

Forests sing with radio signals transferred

Water table "bulges" from radio signals attenuated in crystalline sand

Firmament, morning

Great deep

Chapter Seven

Mechanism for the
Flood

In continuing our study on the panorama of creation, we wish to bring out that, to our knowledge, this is the first time anyone has presented a complete, orchestral creation model.

The original creation was, we believe, orchestrated for the benefit of all life forms: animals and plants, but ultimately and specifically, it was orchestrated for the benefit of man made in the image of God. And please keep in mind that this model is tentative; we were not there to examine the details. But when we correlate the scriptural account with scientific details, they fit together beautifully. We realize that as yet we do not have perfect knowledge, but one day we shall know as we are known. I do believe that we will see the creation concept re-enacted in the coming age, the restored Earth. We will then know perfectly whether these details we have presented are totally accurate. But we are assured that to a great degree they are accurate because of the statements of Scripture.

One of the areas of topical consideration in the world today, and found in all primary records of all the cultures of man, is that there was a worldwide flood at some time in the past. Not only are there records of a worldwide flood in the legends of nations and civilizations of history, but over five hundred cultures have left writings or oral records relating how a few people survived the flood. The names of the individuals surviving the flood have been related in these records. For example, in the chronicles of Babylon, the gods were said to have told a man to build a boat with nine decks, and to fill it with cattle, wild beasts, and food, because the world was to be destroyed by a flood. After a rain lasting six days, according to the Babylonian record, this Chaldean Noah sent out a dove, a swallow, and a raven. Again, according to the ancient Babylonian account, when the man left his ship he offered a sacrifice, and the gods were so pleased they made this man and his family gods also.

In an ancient Greek legend, a man made a box in which he put all the things necessary for life. The story continues to relate that the god Zeus sent a great rain, and the man and his wife closed themselves in the box. Everyone else died in the flood, except those who could climb on top of the highest mountains, and after nine days and nights the rain stopped and the man and his wife left the box.

In India, there is a traditional account of a fish named Mannu that warned a man about a flood that would kill everything. The man built a boat and only he was able to escape.

Dr. John Morris in his book, *Noah's Ark and the Lost*

World, recounts many of the legends and traditions of past civilizations about a flood that killed all the people in the world, with the exception of a few souls.

In all the various accounts by different nations, races, and languages, the essential facts relating to a great deluge correspond with the biblical record. In legend after legend, in report after report, the collective evidence is that there was a flood that covered the Earth and there were only a few survivors.

To continue and mention a few additional traditions relating to the flood, in America the Lenni Lenape Indians believed that there was a time when a powerful snake made all the people wicked. The snake caused water to destroy everything, according to this Indian legend. But on an island there lived a man named Manabozho, the grandfather of all men, and he was saved from the flood by riding on the back of a turtle. While the story is different from the account of Noah and the ark in the Bible, the basic details are the same.

In Peru the natives handed down a story from generation to generation which tells about a shepherd and his family. It was noticed one day, according to the narrative, that their llamas were sad. Upon investigation concerning the despondent animals, the family learned from the stars that a great flood was coming. The shepherd and his family climbed a high mountain, and as the waters rose the top of the mountain began to float, so they were saved.

In the South Pacific natives told how a fish hook got caught in the hair of an ocean god. The god awoke in an angry mood and decided that all the people should be killed. The fisherman begged for forgiveness, so the god told him to go to an island where he would be safe when the flood came.

While there can be no credibility linking an isolated myth, legend, or tradition to a literal historical event, in the case of the flood where such accounts are found in five hundred different sources completely around the Earth, the evidence becomes overwhelming. There had to have been a flood, and in the Bible we have the uncontaminated record of what happened. Related myths, legends, and traditions have these connecting facts: the people of the Earth were wicked; there was a great flood which killed everyone with the exception of from one to a few; and those who were spared survived in a boat, a box, or some other type of deliverance.

I can say confidently, however, that the biblical account is the accurate and uncontaminated record of the flood, because it is the only one that can be entirely substantiated and supported by scientific evidence. Dr. Henry Morris, and others, have compiled evidence which shows that a global flood did occur. Professor M. E. Clark, University of Illinois, and Dr. Henry Voss, have formulated a model which shows the global sedimentary context formed by the effect of the moon on the waters during the flood. The academic impact is that there is evidence of a global flood and there is a global association in the laminated layers of sedimentary rock. The intercontinental linking evidence is that before the continents were separated, there was a great flood. Raised beaches and terraces (even on mountain tops), and great beds of fossils are found which show that life forms tend to gravitate together in a time of cataclysmic events. In these fossil beds literally millions, and some times even billions, of life forms are preserved in rapidly hardening litifying stone.

Limestone is calcium carbonate, which is of the same chemical composition as concrete, and it must harden rapidly or it does not harden at all. So, the evidence is that there was a flood; that it was more than a localized flood; and it was a flood of global proportions.

I am frequently asked what caused the flood. My explanation, while tentative, fits the facts under consideration. To begin, we recap the conditions before the flood where there was a canopy of thin compressed hydrogen encompassed by layers of water above the Earth. The atmospheric pressure was greater, as was the oxygen content, in order to support the huge life forms which then existed. Radio waves bearing music from the stars were received by the crystals in the sand and amplified into musical vibrations. The radio waves from the stars would also have affected the water table. It has been found by scientific research that a crystal, such as silicon sand, does a very special thing in the presence of water when attenuated by radio signals. It begins to vibrate, and adjacent water begins to pump, sometimes on a molecular level, through the layers of the silica sand, thus cleansing the water of molecular impurities. This was a marvelous ecological condition: before the flood, there was a continuous self-cleansing process.

The resonating water did something else, as well. In the presence of a crystal, which is being energized by long radio wave signals, water begins to pump, resulting in the rising of the water table as though being orchestrated by the stars. Therefore, at the morning hour before the flood, there must have been a continuous and gentle flow of water from the subsurface upward, resulting in gentle flowing, resonant streams feeding into larger streams. Such a water system would have also resulted in a mist rising up and dampening all the ground with moisture. The mist would have absorbed from the air the abundant oxygen, making all the water sources ladened with this essential life-giving element for all marine life. When oxygen is depleted from the water, marine life suffers, but before the flood oxygen in the water was so abundant that all forms of life which lived in the water grew to enormous size. The environment and ecology before the flood would be what we would call a "paradise."

Within the Earth, as we have already noted, there would have existed thermonuclear mechanics to keep the atmosphere and Earth's surface within an approximate range of seventy-two to seventy-eight degrees Fahrenheit. The Earth's crust was of granite composition from six to sixteen miles thick (as it is today) with huge reservoirs of water retained underneath.

As to the specific causes of the flood, we refer to the Genesis record which gives clear scientific sequence:

> And it came to pass after seven days, that the waters of the flood were upon the earth. In the six hundredth year of Noah's life, in the second month, the seventeenth day of the month, the same day were all the fountains of the great deep broken up, and the windows of heaven were opened. And the rain was upon the earth forty days and forty nights. (Gen. 7:10–12)

Here are listed three things that happened in perfect order:

1. The fountains of the great deep were broken up.
2. The windows of heaven were opened.
3. It began to rain, and the rain lasted for forty days and forty nights.

Imagine the world as it was then, with a canopy about eleven miles above the Earth; the solid shell of granite; the interior with great reservoirs of water, including huge pools of asphalt and oil in the original hydrocarbon, pristine form; and radioisotopic elements perfectly balanced, with a hard core of iron-based material at the center. The Earth would have been similar to the composition of an egg (without the organic material, of course).

Have you ever taken an egg, put it in a microwave oven, closed the door, and pushed the button? If you have not, please do not! The reason is that this simple, small, pure, life-giving egg will literally explode!

Psalm 46:6 states that God uttered His voice, and the Earth melted. We are amazed in our research at the Creation Evidences Museum at the literal accuracy of statements like the one above. God uttered His voice, and the Earth melted. This would have been similar to the atomic melting that occurred at Chernobyl in Russia—a meltdown within a thermonuclear context. Physicists do not even like to speak of a meltdown, because it is a catastrophic condition completely out of control.

The thirty-eighth chapter of Job indicates that in the orchestrated creation the Earth's internal elements, including the radioisotopic elements, were in perfect balance. If these elements were unbalanced, or scattered, there was a grave consequence. But it appears that this is exactly what happened, and there was a resulting ther-monuclear meltdown. God uttered His voice and the Earth melted.

Microwave energy is simply vibrations at two and a half billion times per second. Our voice is a vibratory form of energy, but we do not have the energy, or the power, or the ability, to vibrate our voice two and a half billion times per second. But God has this ability, be-cause He is all-powerful, and He can do anything He wants to do.

With the simple statement, "I have had enough," (whether literal or metaphorical) God could have brought judgment of the flood with his voice. The physical quali-ties of such voice enhancement probably brought a uni-versal microwave reaction. When you push a button on your microwave oven, there is no heat—simply vibratory energy. That microwave energy traps the water molecules, because the water molecule is approximately the same dimension as the vibration spectrum. The microwave energy traps the water molecules and heats them up.

Dr. Walter T. Brown entered this basic model in a com-puter, and he discovered that when the water was heated to two hundred and fifty degrees Fahrenheit, certain things would begin to happen. Dr. Brown found, as in the case of the egg, when water encased in the Earth is heated to two hundred and fifty degrees, that heat adds to pressure, more pressure adds to heat, more heat adds to pressure, etc., and in a matter of minutes, something has to give. In the computer model, it became evident that where the granite crust of the Earth was thinner, erup-tions would have begun, probably in the Pacific area.

If you were to photograph, at rapid shutter speed, an

egg erupting under microwave energy, you could see it in the picture being torn apart at the seams. The egg would be blown apart in small pieces and larger pieces, as in the case with the Earth—continents and islands. Dr. Brown postulated from his computer model that the ripping apart of the Earth at the seams before the flood would have occurred at two and one-half miles per second. He found that it would have taken only eight minutes to rip the Earth into continents. They would not have been separated at this time, but simply ripped apart at the seams.

Dr. Brown also found that the computer analysis revealed that when the Earth ruptured, water would have been expunged in a narrow band of jet streams with such force it would have erupted seventy miles high.

In a previous chapter, I noted that the only way the crystalline compressed hydrogen canopy could have broken up was by moderating the temperature. Therefore, when the fountains of the deep were broken up, water in streams heated to two hundred and fifty degrees Fahrenheit, or hotter, was thrown up against the canopy, ripping holes or windows through it. As the Genesis account describes, the windows of heaven were opened.

The voice of God surging through the Earth at microspeed energy would have created ultravibrations, inducing a thermonuclear reaction inside the Earth. As a result of the water that was heated above the boiling point being thrown against the canopy at great pressure, the canopy was broken up. The heated water moderated the temperatures in the upper atmosphere and then the sun's full rays began to filter through the broken seams of the canopy. Thus, for the next forty days and forty nights the canopy melted and fell upon the Earth in the form of rain. Due to the lines of force at the Earth's magnetic poles, the canopy would have fallen as ice and encased the great mammoths in their tracks.

Therefore, we have a possible mechanism which caused the continents to be thrust upon themselves, resulting in great mountains, as well as a tentative model for the conditions that brought upon the Earth the flood of Noah's day.

Diagram C: MECHANISM FOR THE FLOOD

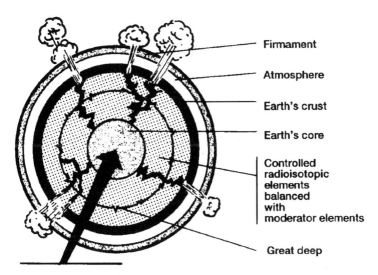

Firmament

Atmosphere

Earth's crust

Earth's core

Controlled
radioisotopic
elements
balanced
with
moderator elements

Great deep

The *VOICE OF GOD* uttered with extreme intensity disrupts the designed balance within the earth. "God uttered his voice, and the earth melted" (Ps. 46:6). A literal *thermonuclear meltdown* ensues from the consequential imbalance. (This is compared to placing an egg in a microwave oven.)

Results:
(1) The violent release of energy causes the waters of the great deep to heat and rupture the granite crust of the earth.
(2) The force and velocity of the hot water breaks windows in the firmament.
(3) The firmament collapses into rain.

Mountain upthrust is a natural succession of events as the violent natural force of the waters thrust the continental granite shelves upon themselves.

Chapter Eight

The Canopy and the
Restored Earth

In preceding chapters I have presented a pictorial description of what the Earth must have been like before the flood. In the days of Noah, there was a superior environment as a result of a canopy, or firmament, in solid form as the Hebrew text plainly declares. It was a world with great atmospheric pressure and oxygen content so that an open wound would heal overnight. To duplicate such a condition for medical purposes is the hope of the future.

We have discussed how the stars shining through the firmament would have been magnified and photo-multiplied with vibrant color. In such an orchestrated environment the radio stars would have sung to man each morning, and the placement of the stars would have provided man with a permanent timepiece, even to the hour and minute during the day. Conditions in the heavens and in the environment energized the plant and animal life forms, and the heart of man rejoiced with contentment in this paradise. The sons of God sang for joy and responded enthusiastically each morning before the worldwide flood.

From the thirty-eighth chapter of Job we believe that all the elements created by God on the third day were in perfect balance. This balance of creation would have provided the Earth with a thermonuclear heater which would have gently warmed the ground and the atmosphere so that at night the temperature would have been about seventy-two degrees Fahrenheit, and about seventy-eight degrees Fahrenheit during the day. All of these environmental factors would have produced optimal circumstances in which man could live. Where there is no ultraviolet radiation from space, all the life forms respond to a pure chemical arrangement. Today, we have an impure and improperly charged imbalance, and the chemistry is errant as well.

Under those circumstances, we then saw what the voice of God could have done in judgment. In Psalm 46:6 the scripture states that God uttered His voice and the Earth melted. We gave a plausible mechanism by which the internal structure of the Earth would have literally unleashed a thermonuclear reaction with a Chernobyl-type meltdown. The waters, under those pressures which were generated, literally ripped the Earth apart at the seams. The deep water sources in the Earth literally erupted forth into the atmosphere, resulting in drastic and sudden temperature changes. Holes were ripped in the canopy covering the Earth, and over the next forty days and forty nights it completely disintegrated and fell in the form of water.

In Jeremiah 51:15 the prophet, by the Word of the Lord, declared that God designed the Earth by His wisdom and power; He created all of it perfectly. But then, in the following verse, there is a transitional statement. We find that there is now rain, lightning, and a water cycle. Before the flood, there was no rain; a mist went up and watered the Earth. But now, there is a judged ecosphere; we see mountains, snows, and varying temperatures. Things in Earth's environment have certainly changed. However, in the biblical record there is a projection for the future.

Let us now consider the final chapter in the orchestral creation model. In Isaiah 35, the prophet described a world that only now can be understood with any dimension. This chapter corresponds to other chapters in the latter part of the book of Isaiah which tell of a coming Millennium when the lion and the lamb will lie down together. It will be a time, according to Isaiah, that a child with a genetic deficiency will still live to be a hundred years old, yet an old man will fully live out his days. This prophecy foretells a time in the future when man will again have the ability to live for hundreds of years.

In Isaiah 35:1, we find a clarified statement which is very encouraging to us:

The wilderness and the solitary place shall be glad for them; and the desert shall rejoice, and blossom as the rose.

What this means is that the Earth will return to an ecospherical condition as existed before the flood. The only environmental factor that could account for such a return to a world like the Antediluvian world would be a literal re-establishment of the firmament. In the biblical record we find the condition for the reforming of the firmament for the restored Earth.

In considering further the promises for a future world, we ask: "Is it literally possible that the wilderness will actually rejoice and sing?" My answer is an emphatic, yes!

In preceding chapters, I have described conditions on Earth under the crystalline canopy and the longwave radio energy from the stars, and how the radio energy would have been transferred to the silica. Man was serenaded each morning by the sand under his feet. Sand actually has the ability to sing when energized, and this fact has been verified by numerous scientific studies. In addition, the atmosphere would be charged with vibrations and resonate within the cellular structure of the plants. Actually, before the flood the wilderness would sing as the Bible affirms. And the botanical life forms would pick up the music vibrations. Thus, the desert has cause to rejoice because of the sand resounding the music of the stars. As the text of Isaiah 35 declares, even war-torn Lebanon will be a place of joy in those days, and the song of glory of the Lord will be sung even by the roses from Beirut, to Mt. Carmel, and to Sharon.

It is difficult for us today who have a multitude of environmental problems to envision such a beautiful scenario. But scientists have discovered that, under certain circumstances, in some of the sands when resonated, there are actual discernible musical notes and harmony in the atmosphere.

Say to them that are of a fearful heart, Be strong, fear

not: behold, your God will come with vengeance, even
God with a recompence; he will come and save you.
(Isa. 35:4)

The indication in this verse is that God will build a context which will be beneficial to man. Man is now in full deterioration. While in the twentieth century science has made a thorough investigation into the functions of life, the environmental dangers causing such diseases as cancer are increasing and encompassing us at a very alarming and negative rate.

Then the eyes of the blind shall be opened, and the
ears of deaf shall be unstopped. Then shall the lame
man leap as an hart, and the tongue of the dumb sing:
for in the wilderness shall waters break out, and
streams in the desert. (Isa. 35:5–6)

The inference is very strong here that the natural circumstances of the ecology will be changed and revert back to conditions strikingly similar to pre-flood days. Man will respond physiologically, and there will seemingly be genetic corrections or repairs. I realize that this is an astounding thought, but at the Creation Evidences Museum we are in the process of building the world's first hyperbaric biosphere to simulate conditions before the flood. Advance studies suggest that if a biological organism is permitted to live within the context whereby it is resupplied with energy without contamination, it has the ability to repair itself to a great degree. Of course, this life-encompassing context includes energizing daily with the right spectra of light, and the correct levels of pressure, oxygen, nitrogen, and carbon dioxide, as it was originally designed to have. In such a reconstituted world where the body will not have to play "catch up" all the time, we can easily envision the coming day of fulfillment for man, as prophesied by Isaiah.

Dr. Robert Gange relates that certain laboratory studies show there is an ability within the DNA to actually strip out inharmonious properties and, to some degree, repair the DNA. If that be the case, it would certainly be plausible within a given ecological context, where life organisms are within their designed environment, for the body to have the ability to repair itself. The blind would be able to see; the deaf would be able to hear; the lame would be able to walk. Programmed within a man's body are the genes composing the entire genetic structure for shapes, sizes, and functions of all organs. Thus, if man's body would be permitted to repair itself, the errant genetic flaws would be corrected and brought back into balance. The designed context for man's optimal benefit was the pre-flood environment under the firmament. A natural corollary for man's genetic expression involves the restoration of the canopy for the Millennium.

I am sure that some will wonder about the mechanics of restoring the canopy, and ask how it could be possible. In preceding chapters, I presented discussion relating to the sustained magnetic field around the Earth under the canopy. As noted previously, Dr. Thomas Barnes and others have found that every fourteen hundred years the Earth's magnetic field would have been at Utopian context where it would have held water vapor or additional substances within its power. If there is to be a replacement of the canopy in the future, a prerequisite is the restoration of the energy in the magnetic field in order for water to be held in place.

In the biblical record, a statement is given that now has an astounding, physical impact on the world's ecosystem. Assuming that the Bible indicates the original firmament above the Earth will be restored, there will first have to be the restoration of the energy and power of the magnetic field. In 1 Corinthians 15:51–52, the Apostle Paul made an illuminating statement:

> Behold, I shew you a mystery; We shall not all sleep, but we shall all be changed, In a moment, in the twinkling of an eye . . .

In eschatology, what Paul referred to was the coming Rapture of the Church, the resurrection, and translation of the saints at the time Jesus Christ returns to Earth.

What was of particular interest to me was that not only will the Rapture occur very quickly, in a moment, but a special emphasis is added—"in the twinkling of an eye." We have previously assumed that this was simply an added statement to impress upon us the rapidity of the event. Three one-thousandths of a second is required to blink an eye, and we have assumed that Paul used this reference to time as an apposition. But the words used in the Greek text give a clearer meaning. The word used in the Greek for "twinkling" is *rhipto*, and one of the meanings of this word is "flashing or rush light." Usage of this word could also include, in contemporary language, a nuclear flashing or atomic event.

Here we have a context of eschatological events consummating with the coming of Jesus Christ. Jesus Christ on Earth had the ability to glow at will. In the first chapter of Revelation, Jesus is described in eternal glory as "the sun shining." Imagine, if you will, the sun being brought within the atmosphere of the Earth. There would be an immediate burst of energy and light that would be detected around the entire globe. The sun has longwave beneficial rays of energy, but it also has destructive shortwave energy rays and devouring heat. But Jesus Christ always does things well. As "the sun shining in all its strength," Jesus did not destroy the Apostle John who knelt at His feet. Jesus did not destroy Peter, John, and James on the Mount of Transfiguration. So the brightness that emanates from Jesus at the Rapture is not the harmful solar energy. His radiance toward His saints would involve beneficial longwave energy, while His display toward His enemies is that of a consuming shortwave sword.

In 1 Thessalonians 4:16–17, we find another illuminating statement:

> For the Lord himself shall descend from heaven with a shout, with the voice of the archangel, and with the trump of God: and the dead in Christ shall rise first: Then we which are alive and remain shall be caught up together with them in the clouds, to meet the Lord in the air. . . .

Underline in your Bible "meet the Lord in the air." If Jesus Christ were to come in His resplendent glory into the atmosphere just long enough to say, "Come up hither," there would be tremendous repercussions. Christians would be caught away; the dead would be charged to life again. On the Earth, the residue of His presence would be sensed. The Bible speaks of "the power of his resurrection," and promises that by the same power the dead will be raised to life again. So when Jesus releases resurrection power at His coming to rapture the Church, it is entirely possible that the Earth's magnetic field is recharged and the environment begins to change in anticipation of His bringing in the Millennium.

Beginning with the sixth chapter of Revelation, we find such statements as the vials of the wrath of God being poured out upon the Earth. Each of these judgments would also add a recharging to the atmospheric context. In Revelation 16, the account of an earthquake is given such as the world has never seen to this time. Every mountain will be gone, possibly leveled, and every island will disappear. Before the worldwide flood, the topography of the Earth had gentle, sloping elevations. The mountains were created at the onset of the flood when the mountains of the deep were broken up, producing great upheavals. Also, the land mass of Earth was not divided into islands. The Earth was not divided until the days of Peleg. So once again, after the Tribulation, the Earth will be one great connecting ocean and one large connecting continent.

At the eruption of Mt. St. Helen's several years ago, water vapor was thrown fifty thousand feet into the atmosphere. Dust was propelled thirty thousand feet upward. When the magnetic field around the Earth is supercharged once more, water will be thrown up into the atmosphere by earthquakes and accompanying volcanic action much higher than fifty thousand feet. It will be held by the increasing strength of the magnetic field until frozen into place as a continuous sphere of ice.

Revelation 16:21 speaks of hailstones weighing up to one hundred pounds, each falling upon men all around the world. Thrown up with the water above the Earth will be billions of tons of dust particles, but all such materials will combine with water as hailstones so that nothing will be left in the higher atmosphere but pure water. The electromagnetic charges of dust particles combine with water normally to cause hailstones. But the hailstones that will fall during the Great Tribulation will be larger than any the world has ever experienced before. This gives us an indication of the awesome power within the Earth's electromagnetic field at that time.

The pure water left in the upper atmosphere will need to be crystallized to provide the benefits described in the thirty-fifth chapter of Isaiah. I believe that Jesus Christ will take care of this also when He returns at the end of the Tribulation in power and great glory. The entire Earth, including the firmament and the environment, will be completely energized by His presence. The hydrogen elements necessary for the canopy will again be bound together and there will be *raqia* to complete the restoration of the Earth to its pre-flood condition.

Jesus Christ will return to establish His Kingdom on Earth, to reign and rule with us for a thousand years. His energizing presence will bring stability, peace, health, and prosperity to the nations of the world. Scientific evidence supports this beautiful orchestration of creation and design.

WHY DO MEN BELIEVE EVOLUTION AGAINST ALL ODDS?

Why do men believe evolution against all odds? As creatures of intuitive reflection, we naturally want to know the answer to "Who or what started all of this?" Evolution has never been demonstrated as a viable explanation for life origins and cannot be supported scientifically. Furthermore, naturalistic evolution cannot be harmonized with special creation. Evolution requires an original miracle of stupendous proportions. The tenets of evolution are insisted upon AGAINST OVERWHELMING AND IMPOSSIBLE ODDS, and its justification exists only in the minds of its adherents.

In this book, Dr. Baugh takes the reader through a comprehensible scientific journey that shows in contrast that special creation recognizes the scientific principle of cause and effect, explores the handiwork of the Creator, and acknowledges that "of Him," "through Him," and "to Him" are all things.

160–page book   •   full-color illustrations   •   hardback

VIDEOS BY DR. CARL BAUGH

Carl Baugh, Ph.D., is the director of the Creation Evidences Museum of Glen Rose, Texas. In these videos, he takes you on an incredible journey starting with the beginning of our universe right through to the coming restoration of all creation, all the while challenging popular evolutionary theories and answering age–old questions about our very existence. Dr. Baugh presents astounding facts about our past, present, and future, in conjunction with the biblical record and provides concrete scientific evidence that secular science has overlooked and has trouble disproving. These video series are sure to make excellent additions to the academic classroom, church bookstore, and especially your home library.

CREATION IN SYMPHONY

Tape One: Evolution Won't Work: Design from the Beginning

Tape Two: Life and the Music of the Spheres; Footprints of a Supernatural Agency

Tape Three: Wonders of the Creation; The Flood, Noah's Ark, and the Restoration

3–DVD Set

CREATION IN SYMPHONY: The Model

Tape One: First Cause; Creation in Symphony; Life by Design

Tape Two: The Flood; Universal Discord; The Restoration

2–DVD Set